The Soldiers Manual

A Guide to Becoming a Believer in Christ.

Pastor Loretta Tanner - Coleman

The Soldier's Manual

A Guide to Becoming a Believer in Christ

True Holiness

Becoming a newfound believer in Christ can be a little confusing in knowing what's the next step or what it all entails. This manual will help answer a lot of your questions.

~Senior Pastor Loretta T. Coleman

Dedication

Bishop Sylvester Tanner

(In Loving Memory)

Evangelist Minnie Tanner

Contents

Introduction to New Life

*C*ONGRATULATIONS! You have now enrolled into the army of the Lord, you have become a part of the Church and have a newfound relationship with Jesus Christ. This is the best decision you could have ever made in your life. Why?

Keep reading…

Not only will you have a better life here in the earthly realm, but you are also guaranteed eternal life in the Heavens here after by following the steps outlined in this book. Just know that this is not a decision of yours. God chose you before you chose Him. Yes, He has always had His eyes on YOU! That's exciting news to know that God Almighty, Creator of Heaven and earth, has always had you on His mind. He began to work on your heart and change your mind to bring you to this point of decision today. In other words, He has given the most important invitation you will ever receive in life, even though you may or may not recognize it now. And because you have accepted His invitation and received Him as your Lord and Savior, we pronounce you "saved."

"Hold on, what does that really mean?" I'm glad you asked, the next few pages will answer a lot of your questions and bring some clarity to this newfound walk in Jesus Christ.

What Is the Meaning of Saved?

To be "saved" means that you have a relationship with God that you have never had before, and you now have access to Heaven when you leave this life. It means everything you have done wrong (your sins) is forgiven. As far as God is concerned, you are free. You are now ready to find out how God wants you to live your new life here on earth, and you are willing to do it His way. He will continue to take care of you, look out for you, and be the Father and Friend you never had before, forever. Your future looks bright, and everything will be alright. You have found a spot in Heaven. But please don't get me wrong, you will still have hard times and tough situations just like you had before you came to Christ. The difference is your going through is no longer in vain, but for the glory of God, and He's with you every step of the way, guiding you through your prayer life.

We have to go back a little in order to fully answer the question, "What does it really mean to be saved?" We believe that we were created by God, and we are not just a mistake or accident of the universe. God had some rules in place in order to make His creation the very best it could be. It's just like when you buy a new car, the manual comes with the car explaining how it operates. This ensures that the car does what it's designed to do at its highest potential. God knows exactly how He made us. He wanted us to be all that He created us to be and to have a great love relationship with Him.

He created us with a free will also. That means that we can choose who or what we want to serve. We have no clue why God created us to have a free will. However, no one wants to be in an involuntary relationship. He could have made us all robots obeying His every command, but our choice allows us to volunteer and show our love to God, our Father. Unfortunately, we do not always choose to serve God. Well, neither did the first man and woman He created. They chose to disobey the very command God had given to them, and since then, every one of us has made the same choice. When Adam sinned, sin entered the world, bringing sickness, war, poverty, neighbor against neighbor, people hurting themselves, and death (Romans 5:12 NLT). Adam's sin brought death, so death spread to everyone.

In our society, when you break the law there are consequences. In some cases, those consequences carry the death penalty. It's the same in God's society (which the Bible calls the Kingdom of God). Whatever we choose against God causes us to be separated from Him forever, but God loved us so much that He wanted to make a way for us to reconnect with Him. So, God had a plan, and that plan was for Him to become a man Himself. This man is Jesus Christ, and He is the Son of God. He paid the price for us to be free and to gain relationship back with our Heavenly Father in spite of the laws and commands we broke and did not keep. Jesus was a blameless man without sin who came to the earth, taught us how to live life, and performed many miracles to prove He was the Son of God.

When God decided to bring us back in a relationship with Him through His Son Jesus, He desired to do so much for us. He wanted to forgive our sins, heal us, and give us everything we needed to live a successful life. God's plan was to protect us, rescue us from our bad habits, and free us from the devil. You know that evil spirit that causes us to say and do bad things. God wanted us to live in love and peace among each other and to know our purpose in life until the end of time when He would bring us back to Himself and we would live forever in Heaven (paradise). So even now, when we make bad decisions, all we have to do is go to God with a sincere heart and ask Him to forgive us, and He does because Jesus died for our sins. We're able to live a new life because after Jesus died, He rose from the dead and went back to Heaven with God (His Father). So by reason of belief, this pronounces us "saved."

Now you don't have to fight your own battles anymore, you have someone to fight for you, protect you, and help you be free from all your bad habits. You also have access to emotional and physical healing through God's power as well as having your needs met in life.

There are four things you should have already done to make this process happen for you: confess, believe repent, and accept.

To **Confess** means you are simply admitting to what you have done wrong in your life and that He is your creator, the only One Who can make it right for you. You are agreeing that you need His help to go through the transition of change and live the right life in Him. You have come to the realization that Jesus is Lord over your life and Satan no longer has rights to you (unless you allow him). You are now rightfully God's property, and you are willing to give and live your life for Him. You are now ready to walk in His will and not yours. But that does not mean that Satan will give up the fight, but with the help of God, you can be successful in your walk in Christ.

To **Believe** means that you have faith in the fact that there is a God, and He's not dead but surely alive, and He is the creator of all things whether it be in Heaven or on earth. It becomes more than just a belief that sits in your mind but has become alive in your heart, knowing that your entire future is at stake, so it's a must that you believe wholeheartedly.

To **Repent** means there has been a complete turnaround in your life starting in your heart and mind. It means you are sincerely sorry for the things you have done throughout your life, and with the help of God, you are now willing to turn away from all your wrongdoing. Turning away is the real test of your salvation. There should be a change, and you should feel a change from the inside out, no longer having the desire to do any of the wrongdoing you use to do. There will be a part of you that will want to do the things you use to do, but the real part of you that you have tapped into has the power to say "No." You will realize the old you was never right, and it could never make you happy.

To **Accept** means you are giving Christ Jesus permission to come into your life, change your heart and renew your mind. Jesus will not force Himself on you, but if you allow Him into your life, He will come in. He no longer has to knock on your door. You have finally opened it, and what He wants to do for you is beyond your imagination. You have accepted the newfound relationship with Him. You accept His words in your heart and believe in your spirit that He is Lord.

When all four things are done and you truly acknowledge them, then you are saved.

Water Baptism

Baptism means to submerge. This is something Jesus asked us to do as a symbol of us dying to our old life, being cleansed and rising in newness. Going down into the water represents a cleansing. When coming back out of the water, it represents new life in Christ Jesus. It is symbolic of Jesus' death and resurrection. When He rose, He rose to new life, and we now have a new life in Him.

Chapter 2

What Takes Place Now?

There should be a change occurring in your life now that you have accepted Christ in your life. You are saved, and if you were sincere, you will notice the wrongdoing you use to do like cursing, using drugs, drinking alcohol, or participating in sexual, criminal, or wrong behaviors etc. are things you will feel different about trying again. Perhaps you have always known something was not right about what you were doing because you were taught better, but being saved, you should find yourself losing interest in those things and a sense of conviction if you try to go back. This can be a difficult process because you may start to feel like two different people. There is the newfound you that has a relationship with God through Christ Jesus, then there is the old you, the person you were so comfortable with before you got saved.

Now you are feeling the change on the inside through God's Spirit, which is called the Holy Spirit. You have now tapped into the real you, the part of you that has always wanted God. The process begins, it's like your body, your thoughts, habits, emotions, feelings attitude, and behaviors are going through a metamorphosis. The Bible calls that portion your flesh or sinfulnature. This is where your desires, cravings, and passions are becoming more and more like God.

Becoming a New Person

Transformation from the inside out is what is taking place as long as you do not resist. Everything that is conflicting with the new person will have to stop. This can sometimes be very frustrating, because the process may feel like war, the spirit on the inside desires to do right, and the flesh is determined to do wrong. This is where you will have to fight to do what is right in order to win. God is working at His best in your life, so don't pull away. Keep moving forward and allow Him to change your mindset. You can stop all the fighting, lying, cheating, porn, sex outside of marriage, homosexuality, gossiping, partying, and drug use of any sort etc. You can do it with the help of God.

While going through this process, you may have slip-ups and make mistakes along the way. When you do, ask for forgiveness and move forward. Do not allow the enemy to tell you, you are not saved. You are saved and have become free through Jesus' precious blood. The struggle is real, but through faith and your fight, everything will be alright. Most certainly a life of sin cannot be the life you live anymore. Taking one day at a time and speaking positivity in your new life is crucial because your adversary (the devil) seeks to devour you. The next chapter will explain Christian living.

Developing a Relationship with God

Developing your relationship with God is very important. Remember, we are made in His image and in His likeness, so we have to get to know who we are and the relationship that's designed for us through knowing Christ. The more time you spend with Him, the more you will experience, and the more He will tell you and show you. Talk to Him, find out what He likes and what makes Him happy. Having a friendship with God is the most important thing you will ever experience in your new life. He's right there to help you make the right decisions and meet all your needs. He will stand with you when no one else will. He will strengthen you and give you hope at the roughest times of your life. He will never leave or fail you. This is not to say He will do everything for you when you want Him to or you will never get angry with Him at times. But when you are done being angry, He's still God, and He waits patiently until you're done being angry, (just don't let angry fester too long) and then He says, "Now let's pick up where we left off."

Understand, in any relationship you will have times where you will get upset and times where things are fine, but working through it and talking things out builds stronger relationships. It's the same with God. He looks for you to talk to Him to build this newfound relationship so He can help you work through and understand certain things you have been through in life. God wants a relationship with you.

After He created everything in the Heavens and the earth, He saved the best for last, which was mankind. There was a closeness between God and the first being (Adam), but sin caused a separation between them and then ultimately mankind. The only way to come back into union with God was through a sinless man, Jesus Christ. When you talk to one, you talk to the other. Many don't understand, but when we pray, we are praying to our Heavenly Father, and Jesus made it possible by dying on the cross for our sins so that we're able to come before Him again, united as one.

But that's not all! There's one more person in this relationship and that is the Holy Spirit. It may sound a little confusing at first, but the more you talk to Him, (developing your relationship) the more you will understand. No matter how messed up we are, He's listening and waiting for us to come back into relationship with Him. How awesome is that? We will learn more about the Holy Spirit in a later chapter.

Developing relationships with other believers

Finding a new relationship with other believers is not hard, but what will be difficult is letting go of some old relationships from your former life. You must look at it as once you become saved you don't do the things you use to, so a lot of old friends will not understand and support your new relationship with God. You will find that they will either be drawn to the Christ inside of you or be drawn away in their sin. This is why God will connect you with believers that believe as you do.

These relationships become a support system. The Bible called a group of believers the church. It's the will of God for us to be a part of the church, which are the believers in Christ. The believers (which is the church) are to become your newfound family in Christ. Some people are more family-oriented than others, but just know everyone is not the same, and everyone is continually growing in God. We are all fighting to get to one place, and that is Heaven. We may have differences and may not see everything eye to eye, but if we stay before God and pray to Him to solve our differences, I promise you He will as long as we're not standing in the way. Just as family members may have disagreements, it is ok to agree to disagree with other believers. However, it shouldn't cause you to leave your church. Remember everyone in your family is not perfect, and neither is your family in Christ. We should all be striving for perfection in Christ Jesus.

Showing love, mercy, and compassion toward each other produces growth in the church, rather it be a correction, kind word, or a helping hand. It has been said that love begins at home. What a powerful saying. You will see that relationships with others will show you the true meaning of love. Developing relationships in the church help believers come together to get the many jobs of ministry done. To find out your role in church is another form of worship, and many blessings come along with it, including newfound relationships with other believers.

The Need for a Pastor

Pastors play a very important role in your growth. The word pastor means shepherd. As a shepherd leads and feeds his flock of livestock, so does a pastor. In this case, the flock does not belong to the pastor, this flock belongs to God. The shepherd (pastor) is put in place to help guide the sheep where they need to be, and if they go astray, the pastor's job is to leads them back in the fold. However, it's not always that easy. Just as a sheep has to be willing to be led by its shepherd, so does God's people.

A pastor cannot lead or guide you if you don't want to be led and guided. The pastor is called and chosen to cover you in prayer and intercede on your behalf, and that can be any time of the day because the pastor is led and directed by God. The pastor is also called to bring understanding to the Word of God and things you may be going through in life that you haven't quite figured out why.

This is not to say the pastor will always have the answers, but God can give the pastor insight into your situation. The pastor is the mouthpiece of God and is called to stay very close to God in prayer. The pastor is to help you find your way in ministry, discovering your newfound purpose in your newfound life in God. So, yes, a pastor is much needed, but ask God where you should attend church and whose leadership you should be under. Everyone cannot be your pastor, so allow the Holy Spirit to lead you to the right one, as you follow them as they follow Christ.

Chapter 3

The Extra tools

This chapter will talk about the tools you need to keep in your spiritual belt. As a carpenter is called out in the field to work, he cannot do the job unless he has all of his tools. Well, it's the same in this newfound walk in Christ. The tools you're about to read about are essential to spiritual growth and life in general. But most of all, it pleases your God in Heaven when you use these tools. They will help you in every aspect of your life. Keep reading to find out what they are.

1. Prayer

This tool is the first tool you want to keep close at hand. You have to have access to this tool at all times. Prayer is just talking and communicating with your God. The power of prayer is going to sustain you. When you break this word down a letter at a time. You will see the reason why this little word is so powerful.

Power **R**estore **A**lignment **Y**es **E**quips **R**ulership

Now let's break this acronym down.

- First, there is **power i**n prayer.

- The power allows things that you have lost in life to be **restored** back to you. You also need to realize that some things were taken from you by God because it would've kept you from this point.

- As the power restores, it also brings you and things in your life back into **alignment** with God. Before you stepped into this newfound life, your old life was out of alignment. God is calling things back into alignment with Him. That deserves an amen because God has your heart in His best interest. So, if this is the case, He is the right person to bring things back into perspective in your life.

- The power of **YES** in prayer also brings things into alignment and causes you to walk in obedience to God, and it helps you find your purpose in life. If you keep a yes on your lips to the Lord, the things that you struggle with will no longer be a struggle in your life, all because of that three-letter word **YES**. And don't just say **YES** because it sounds good, say it because you desire the change that's occurring in your life.

- The power of prayer will **equip** you for where God is getting ready to take you. There are some things that God has hired you to do before you ever knew it. Perhaps its street ministry, jail ministry, hospital ministry, preaching, teaching, singing, or administrating, but know that He will not send you out without the right tools. In some cases, God will give us on the job training and equip us for what He has called us to do as we go.

- Finally, the power of prayer through equipping brings you back into **rulership** in this life here on earth. In Genesis, the Bible says that God gave mankind dominion. Dominion speaks rulership, authority, and power. Rulership comes with your new life in Christ. Everything that the enemy has taken from you, rather it was your mind, your sleep, your health, your love for others, or your laughter, it can be restored through your prayer life in Jesus name.

2. Fasting

The next tool is fasting. This tool goes hand and hand with prayer. Fasting helps to kill fleshly desires and strengthen you in areas you need to be strengthened in. You can fast from anything for a period of time, anything that feeds your fleshly desires such as television, technology, cell phones, music, movies, friends, food, etc. The flesh is your old man, so if you keep feeding the old man, it becomes stronger and stronger. Now that the new man is in place, you have to strengthen it. Let's look at two fasting methods:

- Complete fast: sustaining from food and water
- Partial fast: sustaining from food and drinking water only

These two fasting methods can do wonders in your life if you take it seriously. When fasting, we are looking for results from God. Fasting helps strengthen the new inner man while starving the flesh. You can fast for as long as you want, just make sure you pray and be led by the Holy Spirit before choosing the type and length of your fast.

Some churches may fast corporately, but that would be the call of a pastor or a leader in the church. During the fast, make sure you are reading or listening to the Bible, praying, and lending an ear to Christian and inspirational music for your soul. Remember, the goal is to feed the new man and weaken the old man. Stay away from anything that seeks to lure you back to your old life during this time such as old friends, television, music, internet, and also includes sex with your husband or wife (you must inform your spouse of your fasting period —1 Corinthians 7: 5). During this period, God is working on you as you're allowing Him to work. With this tool in your belt, you can never go wrong.

3. Bible Reading and Study

You may ask why it is so important for you to read the Bible and study? First and foremost, the Bible is essential in getting to know the God you serve, which is the key to having a relationship with the One who died for your sins. You'll find out through your Bible reading and study how Christ was a perfect example just for you. He showed you how to overcome the things that try to tempt you in life. It has been said that the Bible is our map to Heaven. There's an answer in the Bible for every question you have and a solution to every problem. The Bible is medicine for your soul. It was written by a few people chosen by God. The words that were written in each book and chapter were inspired by the power of the Holy Spirit.

You'll find that the Bible is compiled of 66 books in all, 39 in the Old Testament and 27 in the New Testament. You can find stories of men and women's lives, poetry, wisdom, and end time prophecies throughout the Bible. The title of each book, like Genesis, Matthew, Psalms etc., is listed at the very top of the page. Each book has chapters and verses. The Bible was written over a thousand years ago, yet the stories comes alive every time you read it through the power of the Holy Spirit, which is the true Author.

Picking up this tool and reading is not enough. Allow the words to deposit in your spirit and study for more understanding and knowledge. As you do this, you'll find there is instructional, inspirational, faith-built words that will guide you to eternal life. Attending Bible study or Sunday school will increase your knowledge and open up your understanding even more.

4. Praise and Worship

When you come to Christ, your first purpose is to praise and worship God. He created everything to praise and worship Him. The trees, the lilies and every flower that blooms, every bird that soars across the canvas of blue skies, the mountains in their stillness, the ocean and sea in their boldness, and every created thing was all created to praise and worship God. So what would make us any different?

I have a question, if you are not worshiping God, who are you worshipping? Could it be money, relationships, material things, jobs, family members etc.? You would have to answer that question for yourself, but the good news is you are finding out your new purpose and why you're placed here on earth, and that is to give God praise and worship His Holy name. Now you may find this tool a little difficult due to your old lifestyle. But using the other tools in your belt (praying, reading, and fasting) on a continuous basis will sooner or later bring you to praise and worship in your spirit. It's all about developing the tools you did not know you had, because praise and worship has always been there, you've just been giving praise and worship to things and people other than God. Everything belongs to God, and the sooner we realize it, the easier it will be to praise and worship our Creator.

To give you a better understanding of the two, praise is giving thanks and positive expression to His Holy name. Worship goes deeper. Worship opens a very intimate side of the relationship between you and God, and that's what you want. It comes from loving Him from your heart and being thankful for the very things He does in your life. Worship takes you into wanting to change your attitude, bad behaviors, habits, the way you dress, the way you talk, what you listen to, and the list goes on. It's the same way in your old life when you would watch TV and fall in love with certain celebs and sports entertainers. You didn't realize that the love you had for that entertainer caused you to worship him or her.

You hung posters of them on your wall and started to act and look like them. Whatever you did, the love you had for that individual made you want to change things in your life. That's a form of worship. When you worship God the true you comes out, you become overwhelmed with emotions when He comes near and touches you. You start to realize that you have to change for the better, doing whatever it takes to look more and more like God. That is true worship.

There are many ways we praise and worship God. We can dance, sing, play music, read scriptures, pray, clap our hands, and serve others, just to name a few. Being in the house of prayer (church) will show you the different styles of worship and praise. Find a church that operates freely in praise and worship, preaches and teaches from the Bible, and moves in deliverance, which we will talk more about in the next chapter. We all may not praise or worship God the same, but keep in mind, there's only one God that deserves all worship and praise.

5. Tithes and offerings (giving)

Both practices are another way to express your worship to God. The Bible tells us to be a cheerful giver. Giving back to Him in a portion of what He has blessed us with should be gratifying. Understanding that everything He enables us to have all belong to Him. Now that you're saved, you should want to give from your heart. We show our appreciation to God by giving back to Him. The way we show this is by making sure every need is met in His house, church bills are paid, and when applicable, staff members that work for the church are paid as well. His house should be better taken care of than your own. This is the place where you come and fellowship, it must be respected because you love Him and have a desire to worship Him.

Tithing means tenth. The Bible teaches that the first ten percent of our income belongs to Him (Genesis 14: 19-20, 28:20-22, Hebrews 7:1-4 NIV). At first it may be difficult to remain consistent in this area because of other financial obligations, but you will find it easier to commit to tithing if you make it your top priority.

God should be the first person you pay, and everything else comes second to God. Ten percent to God and ninety to your household. If that's not fair I don't know what is. He left us with ninety percent to live on. What an amazing God! Than to top it all off, He gave a promise in the Bible that stated if we do as He asks concerning tithing, He would open the windows of Heaven and pour out blessings we would not have room enough to receive (Malachi 3:8-12). The next part of that scripture says to, "TRY HIM." God is not a God that He should lie. He pours blessings on when you least expect it, and you need to be wise with what He blesses you with.

The offering is whatever you want to give God from your heart. It should be used to fund programs, take care of the poor, promote the gospel so that others are saved, minister to the needs of the people, and if necessary, to build or add to the house of God. He expects for us to give back to those who bless us spiritually and teach us how to live this newfound life in Christ. You can also sow seeds into your ministry or into your pastor when God touches your heart to do so.

6. Service in ministry

Whatever God has called you to do, do it with a glad heart. Serve Him to the fullest. Always give God one hundred and then some. Serving in ministry is something you are called by God to do, so it should always be something you love doing. If you don't know what to do at first, your pastor will gladly assist you in finding the area of ministry best for you. Rather He has called you to prophesy, be a pastor, a teacher, evangelist, counselor, planner, a healer, or feed the poor, you have a tool in your belt that is needed for that ministry. It may seem like a lot at first, but don't let it overwhelm you. All of these tools are much needed and will help you become the faithful believer God has called you to be. So commit to staying diligent in your newfound walk in Christ.

24

Chapter 4

What's Deliverance?

Does deliverance mean the same as being saved? If you look up each word,

- deliverance means *the act of being rescued or set free* and
- saved means *to keep safe, intact or rescue from harm or danger.*

However, Jesus came to save us, so when we accept Him, we are saved. Saved from what though? We are now saved from our old man. We have now stepped into the acknowledgment of our wrongdoing and knowing we are sinners. Jesus came to die for the sinners, save the unsaved, and bring us back into union with God. But deliverance goes a little deeper than that.

Even though God can do it instantly, deliverance is usually a process. Think back to how long you allowed yourself to stay away from God, indulging in your sinful ways, addictions, bad behaviors, and habits. They may have become stronger than you could have ever imagined, but Christ has come to bring deliverance from the things you may have thought were impossible to overcome.

Being a part of a church that operates in deliverance is very important for your complete freedom. Those that operate in this area should be very patient, walking you through and explaining the process to you. While praying for you, the Holy Spirit may reveal to your pastor or the altar worker some things you are battling with. They may call out unclean spirits such as unforgiveness, anger, depression, suicide, fear, or lust etc. The Holy Spirit searches your heart, and with your permission, He comes in and removes anything that's in the way of your growth. That means you must be at a place where you are tired of battling with these unclean spirits, you're tired of feeling angry and depressed all the time or having crazy suicidal thoughts.

In the midst of you surrendering and the leader praying for you, you may feel a struggle between the old and the new man. In my 15 years of experience in deliverance, I have seen a lot, whether in private sessions or in a service. Individuals sometimes experience purging, which can occur from the mouth, nose, eyes, or pores. They may feel nausea or like something is trying to choke them. Coughing and gagging may take place as well as headaches and feelings of pain in different parts of their body. No matter what you feel, keep fighting for your freedom. Whatever is being called out does not want to let you go, but the delivering power through the anointing of God comes to break and destroy ever stronghold.

This is not the time to hold back, just relax in God and trust Him. He has sent His Son to deliver you from everything that has had you in chains. Anger, insecurities, bitterness, resentment, rebellion, stubbornness, worries, self-deception, strife, jealousy, envy, confusion, doubt, pride, addictive and compulsive behaviors, suicidal thoughts, guilt, occultism, witchcraft, sexual impurity, gluttony, false religion, traditionalism, unforgiveness, generational curses that are passed down through your lineage, and the list goes on are all against the will of God for your life. Just know that God desires for you to have love and goodness in your heart, joy, meekness, gentleness in your spirit, peace in your mind, patience, self-control in your soul, and faith that will see you through. Smile, it may sound like a task, but you have someone in your corner, and that's Christ Jesus. He desires for you to be saved and delivered from everything that has had you bound. Just say YES!

Chapter 5

The Power of the Holy Spirit

Now that you're saved, the next step is receiving the power of the Holy Spirit. God wants to fill you with His Spirit, the Holy Spirit. Have you ever heard someone in church say, "Something told me to do that?" Well, that something was most likely the Holy Spirit, sometimes referred to as the Holy Ghost

The Holy Spirit has always been. In Genesis chapter one, Jesus is not yet on the scene, however, He has always been because He's the very **Word of God** (John 1:1-2). The very words that were spoken by God in Genesis one brought things that were formless and void into existence.

But wait, God used His spirit, which is called the Holy Spirit, to reshape, form, and bring things back to life. Matthew 1:20-21 in the New Testament says,

"She will give birth to a son, and you will name him Jesus meaning He Saves because He will save His people from their sins."

Mary was pregnant by the power of the Holy Spirit. As you read further into Matthew 3:13-16 GW, Jesus is being baptized by John the Baptist.

"Suddenly, the Heavens were opened, and He saw the Holy Spirit of God coming down as a dove to Him."

The Spirit of God united as one with Jesus Christ. Jesus performed no miracles, neither was He tested by satan until He demonstrated oneness with the Holy Spirit. The power of the Holy Spirit helps us to overcome test, it leads us, guides us, comfort us and teach us. In Jesus' wilderness experience, it didn't matter how the enemy came, Jesus passed every test. Then He was ready to perform miracles before the people, and ultimately, He was ready to go to the cross for our sins.

Before Jesus went back to Heaven after His resurrection, He promised He would send a Comforter (Holy Spirit) back to comfort us. Christ had to come as an example to show us that we needed power to overcome our old man, which is controlled by satan and his evil spirits. You are no longer on the same team, you have made up in your mind to walk into the new man.

The new man gives you access to the Holy Spirit. The Bible says you have to be saved in order to receive His Spirit. Well, you're here. All you have to do is ask and seek until He fills you. That means you have to get out of your comfort zone, you can't be afraid or shy. Just relax in God.

Being Filled

The Holy Spirit desires to fill you up. The process is difficult to explain because everyone has their own experience. But I can recall when I sought after the baptism of the Holy Spirit. I wanted that Acts 2 experience to occur in my life. Every Friday night I would go up to the church and seek after the Holy Spirit. After two years, I realized my heart was not ready. The enemy had convinced me that the Holy Spirit was not for me. One day I heard a voice whisper to me, "If I was not for you, Jesus would not had died for your sins. The reason why you're not receiving is because you have someone tied to your heart."

I was then reminded of one of the Ten Commandments, *"Thou shall not have no other God before me."* I had no clue I was putting anyone before God until He revealed it that day. That reassured me that Jesus loved me, and the Comforter that He sent was for me. Once I realized that I couldn't take anything old with me on this newfound journey, I started to ask God to remove any and everything that was not like Him, and He did. This is also part of your deliverance. This is part of the Holy Spirit's job to reveal things that need to be revealed. There was such a yearning in my heart to be filled and speak in new tongues as spoken about in Acts 2:1-4.

"[1]On the day of Pentecost all the believers were meeting together in one place. [2]Suddenly, there was a sound from Heaven like the roaring of a mighty windstorm, and it filled the house where they were sitting. [3]Then, what looked like flames or tongues of fire appeared and settled on each of them. [4]And everyone present was filled with

> *the Holy Spirit and began speaking in other languages as*
> *the Holy Spirit gave them this ability."*

Tongues is the evidence of the filling of the Holy Spirit. So, I cried out one Sunday night in a service, expecting the same to occur with me. God had already spoken some words to me that morning and promised me if I came back that night, He would baptize me in the power of the Holy Spirit.

It seemed as if God moved the order of the service out of the way just for me. I kept crying out, "JESUS FILL ME!" Suddenly the power of God knocked me to the floor. I felt a sharp pain in my side. I knew the enemy did not want me to have this precious gift, so I fought even harder. I started beating on the floor and yelling the words God had spoken to me earlier that day, "You said if I came back tonight you would fill me." Suddenly my mouth started to move really fast and my teeth were chattering. I thought, *Is this real?* Within a few minutes, I began to speak another language. I could not believe it, so I tried to stop my mouth from moving, but I couldn't. I realized I needed to relax in God and let Him have His way in my life. It felt as if I was in a warm shower that was soothing every muscle in my body. It was the best feeling I could have ever experienced in life. To this day, I long for that feeling, and God often allows me to experience His power in the same way I did that first time.

You may not have the same experience that I did, but just know you can receive it at any given time while focusing on God, praying, praising, worshiping, or by the laying on of hands. The key to receiving is asking from your heart. The gift (Holy Spirit) is free, however, your old man cannot receive this precious gift.

The price has already been paid for you to receive the full benefits of God. Letting go of your sins brings you into receptive mode of the Holy Spirit. After being baptized with the Holy Spirit, there should be a greater change and hunger after righteousness, and you should recognize it all the more.

Now that you have experienced this powerful impartation, please understand that the enemy does not go anywhere. The fight does not end, and the struggles become even more real. Why? Because the process is not over. It's just begun. God is still cleansing (purging), washing, burning, breaking, and destroying everything that's not of Him. And while God is handling His business in your precious life, the enemy is there to make you think He is not. He may say you did all of that for nothing or look how foolish you look up there. You have the power to shoot those words down. You are no longer eating from his table, step into your new life in Christ Jesus to its fullness.

Get closer to God by using your tools. When the enemy speaks to your mind, pull out your sword, which is the **Word of God** or fall to your knees in prayer. Understand the tools are for your growth and a weapon against the enemy. God has given you the Holy Spirit to help you in life. Learn to consult the Spirit of God at all times. It may be a little difficult at first because of our independent ways, but just know that our independent ways keep us further from God. God wants you to rely on the Holy Spirit, and the more you depend on His Spirit, you'll find that it will become easier, the struggles lessen, and the old hurt and pain starts to diminish, all because you desire to have a close relationship with God through the filling of the Holy Spirit that Christ made possible. All three are one in the same, Father, Son and the Holy Spirit. Without God there could be no Jesus, and without Jesus there could be no Holy Spirit. They work together in unity, one cell, one bond, one church, one God in you.

My prayer is that this manual will give you a better understanding of what being saved means and that you walk into His army in who He has called you to be. Just know you're never alone. If you have any questions, be sure to follow up with your pastor or your church family. May God bless you, and once again, *Congratulations* on your new enrollment into the Kingdom of God!

*Let God think things out for you.

*Let Jesus be the sound of your voice.

*Let the Holy Spirit move on your behalf.

Scriptures of Reference

(New International Version)

Holy Spirit

Genesis 1:1-2

[1]In the beginning God created the Heavens and the earth. [2]And the earth was without form, and void; and darkness was upon the face of the deep. And the Spirit of God moved upon the face of the waters.

Matthew 3:11-12 (King James Version) (John the Baptist speaks)

[11]I indeed baptize you with water unto repentance. But He that cometh after me is mightier than I, whose shoes I am not worthy to bear: He shall baptize you with the Holy Ghost, and fire: [12]Whose fan is in His hand, and He will thoroughly purge His floor, and gather His wheat into the garner; but He will burn up the chaff with unquenchable fire.

John 14:16-19, 26-27 (Jesus speaks)

[16]And I will pray the Father and He shall give you another Advocate (Comforter) to help you and be with you forever- [17]the

Spirit of truth. The world cannot accept Him, because it neither sees Him nor know Him. But you know Him, for He lives with you and will be **in you.** [18]I will not leave you as orphans; I will come to you. [19]Before long, the world will not see me. Because I live, you also will live.

[26]But the Advocate, the Holy Spirit, whom the Father will send in my name, will remind you of everything I have said to you. [27]Peace I leave with you; my peace I give you. I do not give to you as the world gives. Do not let your hearts be troubled and not be afraid.

John 15:26

When the Advocate comes, whom I will send to you from the Father- the Spirit of truth who goes out from the Father-He will testify about me.

John 16:7, 13-14

[7]But very truly I tell you, it is for your good that I am going away, the Advocate will not come to you; but if I go, I will send Him to you. [13]But when He, the Spirit of truth, comes, He will guide you into all the truth. He will not speak on His own; He will speak only what He hears, and He will tell you what is yet to come. [14]He will glorify me because it is from me that He will receive what He will make known to you.

Acts 2:1-4

[1]When the day of Pentecost came, they were all together in one place. [2]Suddenly a sound like the blowing of a violent wind came from Heaven and filled the whole house where they were sitting. [3]They saw what seemed to be tongues of fire that separated and came to rest on each of them. [4]All of them were filled with the Holy Spirit and began to speak in other tongues[a] as the Spirit enabled them.

Your Opponent (Satan)

John 14:30 (rules world system)

I will not say much more to you, for the prince of this world is coming.

John 16:11

And about judgment, the prince of this world now stands condemned.

2 Corinthians 4:4 (controls philosophy of world)

The god of this age has blinded the minds of unbelievers, so that they cannot see the light of the gospel that displays the glory of Christ, who is the image of God.

Ephesian 2:2 (control of unbelievers)

In which you used to live when you followed the ways of this world and of the ruler of the kingdom of the air, the spirit who is now at work in those who are disobedient.

1 Peter 5:8 (opponent)

Be alert and of sober mind. Your enemy the devil prowls around like a roaring lion looking for someone to devour.

Matthew 4:3 (tempter)

The tempter came to Him and said, "If you are the Son of God, tell these stones to become bread."

Revelations 12:10 (accuser)

For the accuser of our brothers and sisters, who accuses them before our God day and night, has been hurled down.

Chosen Scriptures

John 15:16

You did not choose me, but I chose you and appointed you so that you might go and bear fruit-fruit that will last- and so that whatever you ask in my name the Father will give you (according to His will).

John 15:19

If you belonged to the world, it would love you as its own. As it is, you do not belong to the world, but I have chosen you out of the world. That is why the world hates you.

Scripture on Haters

John 15:18

"If the world hates you, keep in mind that it hated me first".

John 15:25

But this is to fulfill what is written in their Law: "They hated me without reason".

Overcoming Scriptures

John 16:33

"I have told you these things, so that in me you may have peace. In this world you will have trouble. But take heart! I have overcome the world."

1 John 4:4

You, dear children, are from God and have overcome them, because the one who is in you is greater than the one who is in the world.

Notes

42

Acknowledgments

Thanks to my loving husband, Billy.

To my handsome boys, KrisShon who was here from start to finish and James Jr. who was very supportive. I love you both dearly.

To my mom who is always praying for me.

To my Faith Temple True Holiness family – I wouldn't want to be anywhere else, doing anything else, with anyone else. I thank God for such a great team of love, unity, and oneness in Christ. The sky is the limit for you all!

To everyone who helped me put this book together. Thank you all for your help.

About the Author

Senior Pastor Loretta Coleman has been in ministry

for 15 years, being first sent to the streets in the slums of Las Vegas to care for the less fortunate. From the streets, Pastor Loretta was called to the pulpit to preach and teach the gospel. Passed down from her father, the late Bishop Sylvester Tanner, a pioneer in the gospel, she is gifted with a powerful deliverance ministry in Las Vegas, Nevada.

Called to operate in a higher call in her personal walk with Christ, the divine power of God has allowed her to realize that much is given and much is required by God. Through the many trials and tribulations on this journey, this woman of God is sold out for the Kingdom of God to preach, prophesy, heal the sick, cast out demons and whatever else is needed for the body of Christ. From young to old, she empowers many through her God given ministry, yet God is going to great measures, still CALLING TO ARMS through the sounds of her voice and …

This is just the beginning!

If you need prayer or would like more information on Pastor Loretta's ministry, you can connect with her through email or social media:

Email: soldiersnchrist77@gmail.com
Instagram: @soldiersnchrist,
Twitter: @soldiersnchrist